Repentance Misunderstood

NA'EEM OMARI

ISBN-**978-0692574362**
ISBN-**0692574360**
Repentance Misunderstood

Copyright © November 2015
Na'eem Omari

Edited by Katrina Avant
Cover Design

Soul Sister Ink
K a t r i n a s w o r k s . c o m

Contents

Connect with Na'eem
@
omariwritings.wordpress.com

Preface

Repentance is one of the most misunderstood concepts in all of Christian theology. It is misunderstood, primarily, because it is not taught correctly. Most of the teaching concerning repentance is incomplete. Most who teach the subject have not studied it thoroughly. As a result, many Christian's labor under the illusion that they have repented yet have not. Without repentance we cannot be forgiven. Without having our sins forgiven, we cannot be saved. How sad it would be, to stand before God in JUDGMENT, believing we are saved, thinking we have done all God requires, only to discover that we have not.

When we study repentance, the way the Bible instructs, we find that there are five steps in the repentance process. These steps are found throughout the Bible and must be put together through an academic study of the subject, as we would any other academic effort. Each and every step must be done. If one of the five steps is not done, then the process is not complete. If the process is not complete, we are not repentant; thus ours sins are not forgiven. Because our sins are not forgiven, we are not saved.

This book is designed to explain the process. Once the process is understood, then each person can decide whether they are willing to do the things that God requires to be repentant. If a person chooses to do these things, God has promised that he will forgive. Once we are forgiven, *then* we can be saved.

It is my hope that someone will be blessed by this explanation of the process. It is also my hope that ultimately many will be saved.

"The position we take on any issue, is limited by our knowledge on that subject. New information quite often breeds a new opinion."
—Na'eem Omari

CHAPTER I

Background

Before we can find and break down the five steps in the repentance process, we must first define repentance, and set out the biblical principles for studying it, as with any Bible subject.

Repentance is the process of getting right with God.

Repentance is a *process*; it is not an *event*. This process lasts a *lifetime*. Each sin requires its own repentance. Each day, for the rest of our lives, we are repenting for the sins that we have committed. This is true, because we have the gift of choice. We can choose not to repent at all or we can choose to stop repenting at any time. God is not in the business of forcing people to repent. However, once the repentance process starts it must go on until the day we die or Christ returns; whichever comes first. This may not seem clear upfront, but when we break down the five steps, this explanation will become plain.

Why must we repent?

We must repent in order for our sins to be forgiven, as we see in **Mark 6: 12,** and **Isaiah 55: 7**. We need our sins forgiven, because any sin that is not forgiven will keep us from being saved. Since all have sinned, (**Rom 3: 23)**, then all need to repent, if we want to be saved.

The reason many Christians believe they have been forgiven, is because they misunderstand how forgiveness works. *No sins are actually forgiven upon request.* I know most have been taught this, but it simply does not work that way. When we ask God to forgive us, that starts the process of repentance, but the process is nowhere near finished.

To grasp the idea of the process, we must remember how God deals with us humans. Whenever we ask God to do something for us that is **beyond our own abilities**, God always requires us to do something that *is* **within our abilities**, as a show of faith. The act is not for God though; God already knows what we will do because God is omniscient. The show is for us. God wants us to know our spiritual condition, so we are not self-deceived; believing we have faith when we really don't.

It is so easy for us to deceive ourselves, because the heart (mind) is deceitfully, wicked, and no man can know it, (**JER 17: 9**). Without Faith though, it is impossible to please GOD, (**Heb. 11: 6**). When we ask God to forgive us, he asks us, among other things, to forsake that sin. If we choose not to forsake the sin, then we have failed to complete one of the steps in the process of repentance. Since you and I don't know whether we're going to forsake the sin, though well intended at first, the process cannot be complete, until we die; ending any further opportunity to sin.

SO THEN, HOW DOES IT WORK?

All requests for forgiveness of sins are essentially held in *abeyance-* suspended until the Judgment. That is those requests are figuratively written beside each sin in the *BOOK OF SINS*, **(Rev. 20: 12, Isa. 43: 25)**, kept by the angels in heaven. Then at Judgment, those requests are granted or denied, based on whether we finished the repentance process for each sin. At that time, it is decided whether or not to forgive us for **each** sin.

Furthermore, it makes sense biblically that sins are not forgiven upon request. Think about it! If sins were forgiven upon request, then there would be no reason for *THE JUDGMENT*, which is an event **(Acts 17: 31)**. *There would be no sins on the books to judge*!

Also, many are confused by translations of the Bible that say God forgave a person. Surface reading suggests God forgave that person *at that moment*. Several things must be remembered as part of the overall study principles.

1.) Most of the Bible was written long after the events occurred.

2.) The writers were inspired by God, and were given insight about future events that had not happened at the time of the event, or the writing.

3.) The original Bible was not written in English. English is a relatively new language and there are word problems in various translations. Often the language being translated to does not have a word with the exact same meaning as the word being translated from. In that instance, the translators used the closest word in meaning. Sometimes there is even a tense problem: past, present or future. To get the full message that God wants us to have we must start with what we have and work our way back. This is why we must STUDY **(IITim2: 15)**, and not just read. Most modern bibles

are a good place to start one's studies,
but are a bad place to stop.

4.) The Bible is thought inspired, not
word inspired. God gave the writers
the thoughts; the words can change
with time, culture and translation.
Pray for, and study, to receive the
thoughts the author was given. Don't
get caught up purely in the words.

Additionally, many think that if a
person believes in God then they are
automatically saved. *This is not true*!
If that were true, then Satan would be
saved also, because even Satan
believes, **(James 2: 19).** The Bible is
clear; Satan cannot be saved, **(Rev 20:
10).** This error is also due, in great
part, to a misunderstanding of **Acts 16:
31**, *and* a failure to *thoroughly study*
the subjects of *SALVATION* and
REPENTANCE.

The book of **Acts: chapter 3 verse 9** requires us to _REPENT_ in order to be saved. The Bible has more to say about _REPENTANCE_ than just what is in one place. All the scriptures on the subject must be put together and reconciled with prayer, to grasp the entire matter, **(Isaiah 28: 10).**

Also keep in mind, <u>REPENTANCE</u> is not like some of the other things God asks of us. Works, for example, are not done **to be saved**; works should be done **because we are saved**. Repentance is different. Repentance must be done **to be saved.**

Now, what are the five steps?

Step one is to _admit we have sinned_. Step two is to _ask for forgiveness_. Step three is to _seek to correct_ the damage. Step four is to *accept the consequences* of our sins. Step five is to *forsake the sin*. These steps are found by searching the scriptures for all they have to say concerning REPENTANCE, and the biblical stories that support them.

Let's review:

REPENTANCE

1.) **Admit** our sins
2.) **Ask** forgiveness
3.) **Seek** damage correction
4.) **Accept** consequences
5.) **Forsake** the sin

A chapter will be dedicated to each step. Keep in mind that all the steps have to be completed to be repentant; and all the sins must be forgiven to be saved. We cannot take any sins into heaven. If any sin is not forgiven, it remains in the book of sins. It will not be covered by the blood, and salvation is not available.

"Confession is liberating; while it may hurt for a moment, it can heal for a lifetime." —Na'eem Omari

CHAPTER II

STEP 1: ADMIT THE SIN

Step one in the repentance process is to *ADMIT THAT WE HAVE SINNED*, **(1John 1: 9).** Without confession of sin, there can be no forgiveness, because there is not repentance. A repentant heart acknowledges wrongdoing, **(Psalm 51: 3-4).** This is why confession is the first step. Without confession, the balance of the process is irrelevant. Besides, why would anyone ask for forgiveness of sin they won't admit they have committed? Equally, this admittance must be real! The best way to explain what is meant by real is to say what is not real.

Some years ago, there was a famous comedian named Flip Wilson. He was famous for his skit in which he blamed Satan for his actions. The phrase he used when he did something wrong was "the devil made me do it". _This is not a biblical admission_!

When we admit our sins, we must take full responsibility for our actions. We cannot blame anyone else, including Satan. Even if someone else was involved in our sins, we cannot blame them. Equally, if someone else influenced us to sin, we cannot blame them for our actions. We are not excused if someone held a gun to ours heads; we cannot cry duress. _We must completely own our culpability_.

Sin in most cases is voluntary. Normally, we knew exactly what we were doing and we even thought about it before we did it. When we admit our sins, we must say to God in essence:

> a) I knew what I was doing,
> b) I knew it was wrong when I did it,
> c) I knew you would be offended, and
> d) I chose to do it anyway.

An admission requires all of the above.

There is a cute little book out entitled "Lord I've sinned, but I have several very good excuses". In this book, the author points out the fact that we often make excuses for our behavior, even when we are talking to God. Generally, we look for anyone and anything that will diminish our culpability when we go to God and ask for forgiveness. However, this will not work before God. We must come with a whole heart; completely devoid of any attempt to lessen our guilt.

We live in a world of excuses. In our courts, we use such defenses as: road rage, diminished capacity, mob mentality; and we even use the Hostess Twinkie defense—I ate too much sugar. But none of these defenses must be tried when we go before God, admitting our sins. If we are truly repentant, we must simply take full responsibility for our actions.

"Contrary to appearances, the greatest pleasures to be gained in life come from denying oneself many of life's pleasures." — Na'eem Omari

CHAPTER III

STEP 2: ASK FOR FORGIVENESS

The second step in the repentance process is to _ASK FOR FORGIVENESS_. One might ask: why do we have to ask for forgiveness, since God already knows what is in our hearts. We must ask to:

> a) Acknowledge that God is God.
> b) Acknowledge God's authority to forgive.
> c) Acknowledge that **only** God can forgive, thus acknowledging God is the only true God that exists, **(Mark 2: 7)**.

Certainly God knows our hearts, the problem is _we_ don't know our hearts. The scripture is clear: the heart, (speaking of the mind), is deceitfully wicked and no man can know it, **(Jer. 17: 9).** Because we cannot trust our own minds, God requires of us some actions that represent where we stand spiritually, as not to be self-deceived. Before asking for forgiveness, the first thing we should do is simply give God his propers for being God all by himself.

When we ask for forgiveness, we must actually vocalize our request. If we are incapable of speaking, then we must mentally say the request. While God is capable of reading our minds, God will *not* read our minds on this desire. If forgiveness is what we want, then we must say it. The act of saying the words, "Lord please forgive me", or something similar, is an outward expression of our inward desire to be forgiven. Remember what we said in the opening chapter? Anytime we ask God for something that *is* too big for us, God always requires us to do something that *is not* too big for us. We cannot grant our own request for forgiveness, but we can say the words in the request.

Equally important, our request for forgiveness _must be sincere,_ **(Ezek. 30: 30-32)**. Many people make verbal requests for forgiveness, but are not really sincere. Keep in mind that you *cannot fool God for one moment.* So many prayers for forgiveness have been offered up, without this mature understanding of _biblical sincerity_. Part of this is because we have not studied to know what biblical sincerity is. King David in the Psalms shows us what it is like to be "heartily sorry".

From a study of King David's attitude when he repented, we see that heart-felt sorrow is a state of such mourning for what we've done that we are physically sick about it, having a broken spirit, a contrite heart, **(Psalm 34: 18)**. This heartily sorrow is such that we cannot stand ourselves for having offended God, **(Psalms 51)**. That's when we know we are heartily sorry.

Many of our requests for forgiveness are offered up quite casually. Then, because we do not understand _biblical sincerity_, we move on, believing we have fulfilled this step, but we have not. Since we have not properly dealt with asking for forgiveness, we have not repented. No repentance- no forgiveness- thus no salvation. How sad it will be for many standing in judgment, believing they have asked for forgiveness for any particular sin, only to find out their request did not meet the biblical criteria.

Next, we have to understand that _at the moment_ of our request, it must be coupled with a _sincere intent_ to forsake the sin. This is to say, at the moment we ask for forgiveness, we plan to fight with all we have in us against repeating that same behavior _forever_. Think about it; what would be the point in forgiving a person for any particular sin, if that person has no plans to stop committing that sin? Many among us verbally asked for forgiveness, _but have no intention of discontinuing the behavior that we are now asking forgiveness of_. This is the classic false attitude about repentance.

In fact, many of us ask for forgiveness while planning to commit that same sin tonight or tomorrow.

I had a friend call me from Los Angeles one day to discuss the Bible. We stayed on the phone for hours. Then suddenly she said to me that she had to ran off and do a list of things (sins), she had planned for that night. I said to her, "Wait a minute. We just studied the Bible for four hours! You told me you wanted to be saved, which means you needed to be forgiven for your sins! Now you're telling me that you are planning to go commit the very sins we just prayed about and ask God to forgive!" She said, "I know, but I will ask for forgiveness before I go to bed tonight".

This behavior is truly classic and common among people who call themselves children of God. Let's be clear, **we cannot ask for forgiveness and expect to be forgiven, while planning to commit those very same sins in the near future**. Step five will deal more with this topic. But for the purposes of step two, we have to understand that at the moment we request forgiveness, we must _intend to lead a new life._

Notice however, I did not say that we would never commit that sin again after making our request for forgiveness. What I did say is that we must _INTEND_ not to commit that sin again. This is where the available blessing of forgiveness is normally abused. Many treat it as if it is a 'get out of hell free card' to be used at our pleasure. We treat it as if we can go sin anytime we want because we know we can simply ask and be forgiven. <u>This</u> <u>misstatement of biblical principle is</u> <u>going to cause a lot of people to be</u> <u>lost</u>! Forgiveness is not available to those who intentionally abuse the availability, **(Heb10: 26).** Forgiveness is only available to us when we make *sincere efforts* to stay away from sin, and on *very rare* occasions failed to walk in the light.

Modernly, this misstatement of biblical principle is so pervasive that most so-called Christians believe we can sin every day, and simply ask for forgiveness that night. If we check the biblical stories, concerning those who loved the Lord, we find that those who did repeat sin, did so years apart. They are the standard. God is no respecter of persons, **(Rom 2: 11).**

We must not allow those who *claim* to speak for God, to deceive us into believing that God is not serious about sin. **<u>God hates sin!</u>** Anyone who teaches that sin is a small matter, and God expects us to sin, is a liar and the truth is not in them, **(1 John 2: 4, Matt 5: 19)**. Quite often these false prophets—modern day preachers and teachers of lies—water down the gospel intentionally, because they are not living the lives God has ask us to live. They spit out such abuses of scripture to take our attention away from their own lives. Beware of such false prophets, **(Matt 7: 15)**. Be not deceived, God is not mocked, whatsoever man soweth, that shall he also reap, **(Gal. 6: 7)**.

"Sanctification is not the result of adhering to a set of rules, but rather the reward of one's faith, which leads us to obedience to God's principles, because we love him." —Na'eem Omari

CHAPTER IV

STEP 3: SEEK TO CORRECT THE DAMAGE

The third step in the repentance process is to _SEEK TO CORRECT THE DAMAGE_. Now this step can get a little complicated depending on the kind of damages caused by sin, but the principles are always the same. Essentially, we must try to diminish the damage we have caused, and if possible, completely wipe it out. These efforts include: apologies, reparations, restitution and anything else that can lessen the harm as much as possible.

Notice however, I said _SEEK_ to correct the damage. In some cases, apologizing to the Lord will be all that we can do. In other cases, there will be things that we can do; but trying to fix it may cause more harm than good. When this happens, another principle suggests that we are to leave those situations alone and let God handle them. Be careful though, we cannot choose to ignore the damage we've done simply because apologizing or repaying will embarrass us. We must ask the Holy Spirit for discernment, as to whether to speak up in those cases. We must not decide selfishly how to proceed.

This is the toughest part of the repentance process for most people. It is the toughest, because while some of us don't have a problem with apologizing, we do have a problem with making amends. When we think about having to give back the stuff gained from evil, we tend to go blind in principle. That evil bounty has often been passed down from generation to generation, and the recipients feel that they are somehow entitled to keep those properties. But nothing is farther from the truth. When we know what we possess is ill-gotten gain, the result of evil, we must not, and cannot keep it.

When we have harmed a fellow human being physically, mentally, socially, or financially, the principles require that we try to put that person in *as good of a position as they were before* we caused the harm. If we stole something, we need to give it back. If we hurt someone physically, we need to pay the doctor bill. If we gossiped or lied on someone, we need to admit that we gossiped or lied; then apologize and tell the truth publicly.

We must do these things as part of correcting the damages.

So why is it important to correct the damages? First, acts of repentance, such as apologizing and paying reparation, are the marks of true sorrow. It makes perfect sense that if one is truly sorry for causing the harm, then that person would want to repair the harm. Someone who is _truly sorry_ for what they have done, will not want to keep the benefits of their misconduct.

Secondly, a refusal to try to correct the harm will interfere with our own relationship with God. Take a look at **Matthew 5: 23-26**. In this text, the principle is made clear that if we do not handle the business of trying to set right that which we have made wrong, God does not want to hear our prayers.

The instruction is that before we come to God with our own prayers and sacrifices, we must make things right with anyone that we have wronged. Then we can come back to God so that he will hear us.

Let's take a look at several scriptures on point. In the book of **Numbers 5: 6-8**, we see how God, through his writer, is instructing us to handle situations where we have offended someone. Notice that in addition to returning the value of whatever we have interfered with, we are told to repay with interest.

Then look at **Luke 19: 8**. Here Zacchaeus, in repentance mode, says to Christ that if he has offended anyone or stolen anything from anyone that he would pay that back *fourfold*. But the affirmation of the principle is found in verse nine. Look at Christ's response. Christ said that he approved of Zacchaeus' repentant state of mind, as well as Zacchaeus' repentant actions. Christ even went so far as to declare that salvation came to Zacchaeus' house that day.

Notice that I gave you biblical examples from both the Old and the New Testament. I do so, because any biblical principle will be found both in the Old and the New Testament. The God of the Old Testament is also the God of the New Testament. Anything that is important to God (a principle) will be spoken of both in the Old Testament and the New Testament. This is true, because God does not change, **(Mal 3:6, Heb. 13: 8).**

Many are confused about things spoken of in the Old Testament, but not in the new, and verse-versa. A thorough study of scripture will show there were practices that were applicable in the OT but not in the NT. Likewise, there are practices mandated by God in the NT but not in the OT. These instructions on how to live, if not in both testaments, were for that period of time and that group of people. These periods are often called dispensations by some Bible scholars. However, the principles governing those rules were still the same.

Likewise, some of the epistles written by Saul of Tarsus in the NT were written to address specific situations in those churches. The rules he recommended for those churches, while grounded in Biblical principles, were for that group, place and time. However, while these rules change with time, place and people; the principles which govern these rules do not change. What is important to GOD now always has been and always will be. *Rules change, Principles don't.*

One last principle before we move to some factual examples. When it comes to offending others, we must categorize them as either *public* or *private*. If the offense is between two people and the public never finds out about it, then the repentant efforts should remain between those two people and God. However, if the offense became public, the apologies and or restitutions should be known publicly.

Why should that be? It is because when sins become public, they don't just affect the two parties. Those who

have observed the sins are also
affected, so efforts to correct should be
made openly. That way, all of those
who observed the offense, or know
about it, can see the Godliness in the
person who is seeking to correct the
harm caused. In so doing, we rightly
represent God and give glory to his
name. On the other hand, if we slap
someone in public, but are only willing
to apologize in private, we have not
met the biblical criteria for repentance.

Now let's look at a couple of
examples. Let's say that you stole
someone's car. Now you want to
repent. First, of course, you want to
admit to God that you have sinned.
Secondly, you want to ask God for
forgiveness. Now, in the third phase of
repentance, you must do some things

in seeking to correct the damage caused. In this case we need to:

> a) Go to the person and admit that you stole the car.
> b) Ask the person for forgiveness.
> c) Give the car back.
> d) Take it back in better shape than it was before you stole it (interest).

If the theft became public knowledge, we also need to go before the church, and or public, to apologize for the sin. These acts show that we are truly sorry for what we have done. It would make no sense at all to apologize to the person, but not give their car back. Likewise, it would make no sense at all to apologize to God, but not apologize to the person. True repentance requires sorrowful action.

Let's look at another example.
Neighbor A's ancestors stole some
property from **Neighbor B's** ancestors
by fraud, deceit and or violence.
Several generations pass and the
descendants have now inherited the
respective adjacent properties. **A** and **B**
are civil. **A** *claims to be a child of
God*, and finds out the property **A** now
possesses was stolen from the
ancestors of **B**, by the ancestors of **A**.
What is **A** to do? This is tough for
most people, because most people do
not want to give up what they have.
Yet, but for the theft, **A** would not
have this property years later.

The biblical principle mandates that
we must not hold on to ill-gotten gain.
Therefore **A** should give the property
to **B,** and apologize for the actions of
A's ancestors. I assure you, this is no

small matter. Such scenarios have happened throughout the history of mankind. Most so-called Christians will not do the right thing in this situation. Yet it is required of us in principle. Also, it does not matter that **B** knows of the theft or if **B** even believes in God. Repentance is about **A**, who claims to love the Lord.

Different situation: What if we stole something from someone or offended someone, but now the person is dead. We cannot give it back to the dead person. We cannot even apologize. The principal says that we should not keep the ill-gotten gain. We must give it to the church, or to the poor, if there is no good church around. Likewise, if the offense was public, we still need to apologize before the church.

However, remember the caveat. If a public apology will cause more harm than good, then we may need to keep the apology between the offender and God. Also remember, the determination of whether to do this must be at the inkling of Holy Spirit. It cannot be ruled by our desire to avoid embarrassment.

Consider this example: If one man commits adultery with another man's wife, the adulterous man owes the husband an apology. If the husband knows, then the apology must certainly be given to the husband. If the whole Church family knows, then the apology must be public. If only the two offenders know—wife and outside man—then it may be best kept between God and the offenders. Apologizing may create more havoc in that home. In this case, counsel with the Holy Spirit is necessary. It may instruct that we give no more exposure to that sin, because the exposure may cause more instability in a home already struggling. Remember however, this is for the benefit of a home, which God loves, and not for the benefit of the offenders.

Some of us may have lied or gossiped as much as 20 years ago that caused someone harm. Oftentimes, relationships have been damaged and we have not spoken to that person all that time. Once we establish a relationship with God, and are in the process of repenting, we then have a duty to go back and do what we can to repair the damages. Specifically, we need to go back and apologize for our part in causing relationships to deteriorate. It may well be that not all the blame is ours. However, what the other person did is between them and God. A repentant person must now be willing to go forward and apologize for his or her part, and ask for forgiveness.

It is not important whether the other person is equally apologetic. It is not important whether our apology is accepted. **A child of God must do what is required, without regard to what others do**. By apologizing for our part, we are getting right with God. Then if possible, God can work on our behalf to repair some of the damaged relationships. It is never too late to apologize for what we've done. Keep in mind that **apologizing requires humility**. God requires that we humble ourselves so he can save us. **(Matt 5: 3, 5)**

All of these things are part of the requirements to try to make things right once we have sinned. These scenarios can vary so greatly that we cannot address each and every one. That's okay though. What we need to know are the principles that govern all situations.

We must try to make things right both with GOD and with the person!

"The most powerful weapon any human can possess is the one that the enemy cannot see." — Na'eem Omari

CHAPTER V

STEP FOUR: ACCEPT THE CONSEQUENCES

In order to explain chapter 5, we must make a biblical distinction for clarity. *There is a difference between <u>consequences</u> and <u>punishment</u>.*

Punishment is what happens to us after the judgment and death. Once all the cases of every human who has ever lived have been thoroughly investigated, the Judgment will be over. When Christ returns, all punishment or rewards will be executed, **(Rev. 22: 12)**, either heaven for the righteous or hell for the wicked.

The punishment for sin is death. There must be a death. The Scripture is clear that the wages of sin is death, and the gift of God is eternal life…, (**Rom. 6: 23)**. However, the good news of the gospel is **punishment for our sins can be avoided**. The punishment can be avoided by giving our lives to God. Once we give our lives to God, his son has promised to step in as a substitute and die for us. That death has already occurred. Christ has already died for the sins of everyone who gives their lives to him. Thus, we can avoid punishment.

Consequences, however, are different. These are what happens to us *during our lives* as a result of sin **(Prov. 11: 31)**. **ALL SIN HAS CONSEQUENCES**. We will reap what we sow, **(Gal. 6: 7)**. Consequences are the natural and or spiritual results of our actions; both good and bad. In some cultures, it is referred to as karma. Because we live under God's natural laws, as well as man's laws, some things will simply flow from our actions. Even if man's law does not hand down consequences for our sins, because we didn't get caught, God's law will cause us to experience consequences during our lifetimes.

Consequences cannot be avoided. Even those of us who will be forgiven for our sins eventually, and thus avoid punishment after physical death, cannot avoid the consequences of our sins during our lifetimes.

So why is there the need for consequences? Since we know God cares about all his created beings, why doesn't God just let us have fun?

First, God hates sin. Sin is disobedience to the very God who has given us so much. What giver would not be offended when the receiver does not show appreciation by doing what the giver asked? We believers say we love God. If that is true, then God has a request based on that statement …*If you love me*, keep my commandments and obey my instructions, **(John 14: 15)**. Then, as to help us not deceive ourselves, God says he knows which ones among us really love him; it's the ones that obey him, **(John 14: 21)**.

Second, sin is bad for us. God made us, knows all about us and knows what is best for us. The things God calls sin are things that will hurt us. Since God loves us, God does not want to see us get hurt. We often don't understand why God declares certain things to be sin but like earthly parents God makes certain things off-limits so we won't hurt ourselves. Such declarations are not acts of idle domination but rather acts of pure love.

Third, God is in the saving business. By meting out consequences, God teaches us the bigger lesson concerning eventual punishment, and tries to guide us into changing our ways so we can be saved. God desires that none be lost, but that all shall come to repentance, **(2Pet. 3: 9)**. God does not hand down consequences because he hates us, but rather he hands them down because of love, **(Rev. 3: 19)**. Those that he loves he chastens.

Fourth, God is so wise. Some questions we humans have will not be answered unless we take advantage of

the plan of salvation and go to heaven.
There we will sit at the feet of the
master and can ask all our questions.
There we will receive all the answers
as we experience the wisdom of God
forever!

Let's take a look at a few classic
examples of the consequences of sin,
even by those who we are pretty sure
will not have to suffer the punishment
of death later.

Consider King David, **(2Sam 11-12)**,
who committed adultery and murder
during his lifetime. Since he was so
highly thought of by God, it is likely
that he will not experience the
punishment of death after judgment,
and his sins would be covered by the
blood of Christ. However, _he could not
avoid the consequences_. If you recall,
even when he finally asked God to

forgive him for his sins, God did not remove the consequences. His consequences were that his firstborn child was to die, and his house would not have peace for the rest of his natural life. **(2 Sam 12:10-23)**. If you also remember, he rent his clothes, and did not eat for a week; pleading with God to alter the consequences of his actions. After one week God did not alter the consequences and David accepted what God decided.

It is important to see, since God hates sin, God cannot allow sin to go on without effect (consequences), even during our lifetimes.

It is also important to see that David had to accept God's decision concerning the consequences of his sins. Likewise, we must be willing to accept God's divine providence when

God decides our consequences. These consequences are for our own spiritual good. It may not seem so at the time, but it is. If David refused to accept the consequences and fought against God, David would be lost.

Consider an earthly parallel. When children disobey, good parents usually issue some kind of consequence. The severity is usually proportional to the degree of the offense. Once the parent tells the child what the consequences are, the child has choices. The child can accept the consequences, knowing the parent loves them and feels the need to teach something, or the child can rebel and act out, refusing to accept the wisdom and love of the parent who has shown them such thorough out their lives.

When a child acts out, refusing to accept the tough love parents sometimes have to show, this offends the parents. It is painful for a parent to know that this child is happy to accept all the food, housing, gifts, money and love that has been given, but will not accept the chastisement stemming from the wisdom of parents, who know more about life than the child. This damages the relationship between the two and may have lasting effect.

Likewise, when we, the child of God, accept all God's gifts—sun, moon, air, health, and the death of his son—but won't accept the chastisement for sin, we damage the relationship _and it may be permanent_. The last thing any good child should want to do is offend a wonderful FATHER!!

Let's look at Moses as an example.
Moses did wonderful things as an
ambassador for the Lord. Yet, Moses
was not exempt from the fact that all
sin has consequences. When Moses
smote the rock rather than speak to the
rock, there were consequences, **(Num.
20: 7-12)**. Moses, as a consequence,
did not get to enter the promise land.
Instead, he finished his journey on Mt.
Pisgah, overlooking the promise land.
Some might question the fairness of
God; it may seem to be such a harsh
consequence after all Moses endured.
Keep in mind though, God knows a
whole lot more than we do, and always
works in our best *spiritual* interest.

Furthermore, Moses is one of the few
humans we are sure is already in
heaven, **(Jude 9)**. Thus, we know the
consequences did not diminish God's

love for Moses, but rather was a result of God's love.

Lastly, in understanding the need to accept consequences, we must examine the duality of our relationship with God. God is both _Savior and Lord_. God is our _Savior_ in that God can save us from death, **(John 3: 16)**. God is also our _Lord_ in that God gets to tell us how to live our lives. **We cannot accept God as Savior, with all its benefits, and not accept God as our Lord, with all its requirements.** None among us have a problem with God snatching us from the hands of death. However, many among us have a problem with God governing our lives once we are saved.

By accepting God's divine providence, in consequence for our sins, we accept God as Lord and all God speaks from that position. When we accept our consequences, we say through actions that we accept God's authority as Lord, and will not fight against his proclamations. Just as children in the physical realm must accept the consequences for their actions handed down by their earthly parents, we the children of God must accept the consequences of our sins handed down by the God of the universe. By accepting our consequences, we show trust in God's wisdom and respect for God's lordship in our lives.

"The beauty of a relationship with God is that we don't have to win to win, we simply have to fight with all our might." —Na'eem Omari

CHAPTER VI

STEP FIVE: FORSAKE THE SIN

The final step in the repentance process is to forsake sin. While it is simple, many struggle with this particular step. We want to be forgiven, which means we understand the need to repent. But, giving up that particular sin is often a difficult thing. It is often difficult because we have fallen in love with that sin.

The idea of not sinning is strange in our world. We live in a world that encourages doing whatever we feel like doing, whenever we feel like doing it. We are so hedonistic that the thought of denying oneself voluntarily is strange at best.

Furthermore, we humans have the additional problem of being born in sin, and shapened in iniquity, **(Psalm 51: 5)**. We are naturally selfish and seek to do what we want to do. Our DNA is corrupted. This corruption within us was handed down from our ancestors Adam and Adama who chose to sin, and then passed that predisposition on down to us. On top of all that, we also have to deal with the fact that many of us have simply fallen in love with certain sins. Anyone who has ever been in love knows that falling out of love is a tall order. Giving up something that one has been in love with for a long time often requires discipline, and determination that most of us are not willing to muster. Our only hope for giving up long cherished sins is to call upon the highest force in the universe;

the one who is able to keep us from falling, **(Jude 24-25).**

Even then, it does not happen just because we ask God to do it. Again, *salvation is a cooperative effort.* Likewise, coming to a place in one's life where we no longer commit certain sins is also a cooperative effort. *God is not in the business of forcing people into a certain lifestyle.* If we want the Holy Spirit to take sin out of our lives, we are required to cooperate with the Holy Spirit and do what it asked of us in the effort.

However, a request for assistance with forsaking a sin will always be answered. This is true, because God hates sin; thus God is always willing to help. Also, God wants as many who desire such, to be saved, **(1Tim 2: 4).**

But, God will not save us without our help.

Imagine a man on a cruise ship falls overboard. He screams out for help, asking to be saved. A benevolent person on board the ship wants him to be saved and throws out a life preserver. The life preserver lands within two inches of the drowning man. All the drowning man has to do is to reach out and grab the preserver. The drowning man chooses not to reach out; rather he continues to wait for someone else to come save him without his own help. That man will likely drown and be lost. God's willingness to save us is much like that situation. God will do the greater part necessary to save us; God will require that we do the small part as to benefit from his greater efforts. If the thing that we're asking for is help to stop sinning, then the Holy Spirit will require our cooperation with specific instructions on what our part is in the effort.

God is an '*IF Then*' God. God says to us through scripture that *IF* we do certain things, *THEN* he promises to do certain things, **(2Chron 7: 14)**. If we don't do our part, then he is not obligated to do what he promised.

For example, let's say that the sin you want to forsake is fornication and you haven't been able to stop on your own. Now, you have asked the Holy Spirit to take it away from you. Then what the Holy Spirit will do is give you special instructions that will assist the Holy Spirit in relieving you of that sin. The Holy Spirit may instruct you not go around the object of your desires. If there's someone in particular who you have been fornicating with, then it is likely that the Holy Spirit will instruct you not go around that person anymore, calling them by name. You might even need to move to another state, with no forwarding address, if you really want to stop. If the sin is fornication in general, then the Holy Spirit may instruct you to stay away from certain places: night clubs, certain recreations centers or some other places. That is the part you will play in your own salvation through repentance. If you refuse to cooperate, then God is not obligated to take it away. Again, God will always require us to do our part in saving ourselves, **(John 8: 11, 5: 14)**.

My grandfather used to say it this way: "God won't give you the soup and the

spoon too. God will give you the soup;
you'll have to get your own spoon."
God will handle the greater part; we
must handle the lesser. No one will be
saved without their own cooperation.

Look at the biblical example of the
woman who was caught in adultery.
Notice what Christ told her to do, as
her part in her forgiveness through
repentance. Christ told her to "*go and
sin no more*", **(John 8: 11)**. If we plan
to continue in sin, we will not
complete the repentance process;
forgiveness is not available.

Again, as discussed in an earlier
chapter, it makes sense that we would
need to work at forsaking the sin, if we
want God to forgive us. If God has no
problem with us continuing to commit
the very same sin over and over again
without any effort to stop, then why

would God forgive us in the first place?

The reason step five is so critical for repentance is because of something that we said earlier. Remember, sins are not actually forgiven upon request. The reason that is true is because when we put our request in for forgiveness of sin, God does not make a decision right then. God waits until the judgment to decide whether sins will be forgiven. Part of the reason for waiting is so that we can see whether we gave our best efforts to forsake the sin, after putting in a request for forgiveness.

So imagine we put in a request for forgiveness of a particular sin on day one, but for the next five years we continue to commit that same sin, with little or no effort to do the part God ask us to do in the process. This is evidence that we were not truly repentant, and determined to quit the sin. It is not required that we never repeat a particular sin again; however, we must put forth best efforts so that God will do his part in helping us to overcome that sin. Remember, we cannot fool God for a moment. God knows whether we have done our best to forsake the sin. If not, then we will not get the help we need from God to overcome that sin. <u>We must do our part!</u>

A key to forsaking the sin is to come to view it, and all sins the same way God does. *Learn to hate sin*. Perspective is so important in handling life's difficulties. If we grow to see a thing as ugly and demeaning, we will tend to stay away from it. If we view it as a repulsive thing that can interfere with valuable things, then we will likely avoid it; even flee from it, **(1Cor. 6: 18)**. In essence, we must take on the mind of Christ. Let this mind be in you, which was also in Christ…, **(Phil. 2: 5)**. We must see sin through the eyes of God. Then and only then will we have a shot at living the way God asks, and be that living sacrifice God requires, **(Rom. 12: 1)**.

"If all we see in life is what we see, then we will always be blind."—Na'eem Omari

Conclusion

As you can see, repentance is not as simple as most people think that it is. Repentance requires that we do some things. Simply saying that we are sorry is not enough. It is a part of repentance, but nowhere near its entirety.

Many among us, who believe that we have repented, have fallen woefully short in that effort. We believe that our relationships with God are intact. Therefore we believe that if we died today, we would be saved. This is the sad part of this erroneous teaching.

Likewise, we cannot blame our lack of knowledge on the fact that we didn't know we had to do all that. The Scripture places on us a responsibility to study in order to know what God requires of us to be repentant **(IITim2: 15)**. We cannot stand before God in the Judgment and say, "my pastor didn't tell me that." <u>**Each of us must study for ourselves**</u>.

Additionally, lumping our sins together in a request for forgiveness, will not work either. Saying "Lord please forgive me for any sins I have committed", won't get it. We must ask the Holy Spirit to bring back to our remembrance the sins we have committed, so we can spend the rest of our lives trying to make things right and, sin no more. Repentance requires all that.

It is my hope that through this writing, many will come to know the steps God requires of us, in order to be repentant. Then each of us can make an informed decision, as to whether we are willing to do what God requires to be repentant, and as a result, be saved.

The Author

Poem

As we travel near and far
We see so many things that are
Remarkable as it may seem
And quickly sits one's eyes to gleam.
But even in the midst of praise
I realize this thing that's made
This world we're in so possible
And the things we see so wonderful.
So be impressed with worldly gleam
And ask thyself what does it mean
But you remember as you stand appalled
That God's the Author of it All.

Na'eem Omari
1978